Salvaged from School fire - May 1979.

Published by G. Whizzard Publications Ltd.,
in association with André Deutsch 1978
105 Great Russell Street, London W.C.1.

ISBN 0 233 96990 X

Typeset by Trade Linotype Ltd., Birmingham,
England
Printed in Italy by New Interlitho (S.P.A.)

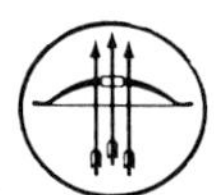

The Facts about a Theatre Company

Featuring The Prospect Company
Introduction by Derek Jacobi

by Peter Lewis
Photography by Robin Constable

Series consultant editor: Alan Road

Introduction

A friend of mine once said that Cinema makes you rich, Television makes you famous, but the Theatre is what it's really all about. My own experience as an actor, my instincts and the reactions of many a live audience have so far proved this summary to be true. The agony and the ecstasy of the theatre are their own rewards – and there is no lack of either in a touring company.

In the following pages of this book you will find, recreated with enormous feeling and perspicacity, the life of a company of itinerant players whose work is no ordinary 'mystery' – but captured here is that mysterious ordinariness of their lives which for centuries past put them into the vagabond class of unrespectability. Peter Lewis, a distinguished and ardent theatre-goer, and photographer Robin Constable, dogged our footsteps for many months, out front and behind the scenes. This introduction gives me the welcome opportunity to thank and congratulate them on a true and affectionate reconstruction of our efforts. The minutiae of an actor's day, of a production from stomach-knotting auditions to stomach-turning First Night, are told with the public concern and the private comment of keen and loving observers. Perhaps, the only element missing from Peter Lewis's description of rehearsal-room, dressing-room, and wings is the 'highly charged' language with which the air is often coloured. Perhaps, he thought to preserve our reputations untarnished. So, I thank him. When the Ghost implored Hamlet to 'SWEAR', Hamlet very often did!

I, for one, am grateful to this book in that it answers fully and comprehensively that age-old question put to many actors (by even the keenest theatre-goer): What do you do during the day? It is as if the magic of illusion, the suspension of disbelief, are so strong that there is no impression of the actors having existed (let alone worked) before the curtain rises. Peter Lewis tells it as it is and Robin Constable shows it as it was. The glamour may be thin and superficial but it is worn with a flourish; Leichner can eradicate a multitude of sleepless nights; Doctor Greasepaint still convinces that your place is on stage and not as you thought, as you tottered to the stage-door, at home with blankets and a hot drink. Not that actors are martyrs, but there is a certain divinity about them, shaping their ends however roughly hewn. We are here described as vulnerable rather than cocky, creatures of superstition and habit, sponges for endless reassurance, haters of critics (apart from ourselves), conjurors of order out of chaos, and mild hypochondriacs.

It's a pretty fair list. To mis-quote Hamlet, they have drawn their breath (in pain?) to tell our story. As far as I am concerned they have reported 'me and my cause aright to the unsatisfied'. I thank them. May you enjoy the show.

Derek Jacobi.

Foreword

To most people who have ever experienced the urge to perform, a professional life in the theatre sounds incomparably glamorous. It is and it isn't.

No doubt to be in a hit show, playing to the applause and excitement of packed houses, is a more stimulating and heady experience, both on-stage and back-stage, than anything that the empty spaces of the film or television studio can offer. When a thousand people are united in concentration on a stage, the players and the audience can establish a paradoxical state of intimacy and rapport for which any amount of privation, discomfort, anxiety and uncertainty is worth suffering.

At least it is so for the addict, despite the profession's dismal prospects, low average pay and the likelihood that at any time two-thirds of its members will be out of work. Apart from these discouragements, a great deal of theatre life is hard slogging for exhaustingly long hours. It is the tedium of repetition, once a show has been run in. It is the ever-present fear of failure and public humiliation if the show is a flop.

It is because of its peculiar exhilarations and miseries and its unsocial hours, that the theatre is such a closed, cliquey, inward-looking profession. For so long treated as outsiders, as 'rogues and vagabonds', theatre people stick together not only at work but off stage. They talk shop continually. When out of work, they live primarily for their next engagement. They have a reputation for egotism which comes more from their insecurity than from their conceit.

This book attempts to describe this dual nature of life in the theatre through the medium of a touring company – the Prospect Theatre Company. It tries to balance its heights and its depths, not forgetting the long waits that occur in between.

Auditions

It is eleven o'clock on a December morning and three actresses, clutching Shakespeare texts, are sitting on draughty benches just inside the stage door of a West End theatre, carefully ignoring each other like patients in a doctor's waiting room. The stage doorkeeper, unusually talkative for one in his profession, is trying to break the ice. 'Oh yes,' he repeats, 'I've seen them all come and go here. Sir Ralph Richardson, all of them.' The girls acknowledge him without enthusiasm. They are preoccupied. In a few minutes they will be auditioning for the part of Ophelia in *Hamlet*.

One by one they are led down the chilly passages to the womb-like darkness at the back of the stage. Somewhere out in the blackened auditorium sits the artistic director of the Prospect Theatre Company, Toby Robertson, his fellow director, Timothy West, and other invisible advisers. From where you stand, blinded by spotlights on the front of a stage that stretches emptily away in every direction, you can see nothing of the theatre beyond the second row of blank stalls. It is a platform in a vacuum. Standing on it you might be disembodied, floating in space.

'Good morning!' calls Toby Robertson's voice out of the darkness. 'You are, let's see . . . ah, yes. What are you going to do for us?' The first actress reads Ophelia's speech to Polonius, describing Hamlet's madness—'My lord, I have been so affrighted'. The words are apt. She comes to the end of it with the leaves of the book in her hand trembling visibly in the lights.

There is a whispered consultation. Then: 'We want you to go on. Can you do something more?' With a look of terrified enthusiasm she says brightly: 'Right! I'll do the mad scene!' 'Good. Will you do the song? It's up to you, of course.' Timothy West's voice cues her in from the outer darkness: 'How do you, pretty lady?' She takes a deep breath and does the song.

She, like the others, is there because her agent was telephoned and asked if he had anyone to suggest for Ophelia in a nine-month engagement next year, and to play as cast in other plays in the repertory. By the time she reaches 'Good night, ladies', at the end of the mad scene, the unseen watchers have probably decided whether she should be offered the nine months. But they will give nothing away. 'Right. Good. Thank you very much for coming along. We'll talk to Ken' (her agent). In the passage on the way to the stage door, she passes the next candidate coming down.

One of the succession of Ophelias explains solemnly that she proposes to play her literally paralysed with grief. One proudly discards the book and then looks as though she wishes she hadn't. Another asks if she can take off her shoes. 'Throw yourself on the floor for all I care,' says the voice out front. At the end of the morning the stage doorkeeper is still reminiscing to his changing audience of three: 'Yes, we've seen them all here. Sir John Gielgud now, I know him very well . . .'

After the Ophelias come the prospective Laertes, the Horatios, the Rosencrantzes and Guildensterns. Auditions run for two or three weeks. A West End theatre has been hired for the purpose during daytime hours. They can use the stage until five o'clock.

Nobody embarks on a production of *Hamlet* without having cast the Dane, the King and Queen, probably Polonius, perhaps the Ghost and First Player (roles which are generally doubled by the same actor). The rest are filled by auditions of invited actors reading for specific parts and some by general auditions which may be advertised in *The Stage,* the profession's weekly newspaper. In this case the company keeps a register of all those who have applied to work for it in the past year – 170 strong – and very honourably invites them all along to be seen. It is a time-consuming courtesy – not many of these are likely to prove useful. In five days, only 25 people emerged who might do.

All kinds of actors apply for Shakespeare auditions, some from steady jobs in the subsidised companies like the National and the Royal

Shakespeare, some who are currently in pantomime or *Oh! Calcutta!* or, more usually, in nothing. Many bring ambitious pieces they have specially prepared for auditions only.

'All right, then, give me your Henry.' They give their Henry or their Richard, their Edmund or their Hotspur, and sometimes a character part with heavy accent and quirky walk. Some positively bound about the stage in a totally unsuitable manner for a minor part. One says boldly, 'I'm going to go the whole hog and do "To be or not to be" ' – undeterred by the fact that he would probably be the first Indian to play the part in this country. No one is humiliated by being stopped in the middle, though there is the occasional reproof – 'I'm getting absolutely nothing from inside. You mustn't waste my time – or yours.'

There is a marked disparity between their ambitions and the parts likely to be on offer. One day, every other actor seems to be doing Cassius, the next day Henry V, but the parts to be filled are likely to be inconspicuous courtiers like Voltimand or Cornelius, or possibly Osric or Fortinbras.

Why go through this long-drawn-out and wearing procedure? 'You can talk to somebody in a room about a part for hours,' explains Toby Robertson, 'but when they get up there and use their body and their voice it may just be hopeless and it's the only way to find that out.'

They are looking for qualities of voice, the ability to speak verse and physical presence on the bare stage. 'It's a great mistake to move around a lot,' says Timothy West. 'The most useful thing to demonstrate is that you can do a six-line messenger speech and hold an audience of 1000 without shouting or waving your arms. The people we want have also got to be versatile and not mind doing a lot of slave work in several small parts for very little money. An actor can make much more money sitting at home waiting to do a few days telly. With us you get a pretty good classical training. You have to choose. But I suspect that 70 per cent of the people we want will turn down either the parts on offer or the money.'

Why, then, are there so many hopefuls competing for anything that is going on the poorly rewarded stage? The reason is that though money may be made in small parts on television or in films, reputations are not. The stage is still the place for that. Casting directors in television still look for their stars among actors of proved experience and reputation in the theatre.

In the third week, the actors marked P (for Possible) on the director's sheet are recalled and auditioned again. They are invited to play scenes with the leading actors, Derek Jacobi (Hamlet) or Timothy West (Claudius). This is unusual. 'I don't like doing it because everyone is so tense and self-conscious,' says Derek Jacobi. 'I hated doing auditions in my time. But occasionally with someone you get the feeling – yes, I'd like to act with them.'

On this occasion he finds an Ophelia. With each of the finalists he plays the 'Get thee to a nunnery' scene with all the stops out. The Ophelia who reacts most capably to being scolded, assaulted, even thrown to the floor, is Suzanne Bertish, an unconventional actress of 25 whom Toby Robertson had been impressed by when she was playing, of all things, a blind Jewish lady of 95 in *Woyzeck* at Glasgow. She is already in a play and has taken a couple of hours off from rehearsals to attend. 'It's very different applying for a part when you are in work rather than out of it,' she says afterwards. 'Other people were far more excited when I heard I'd got it than I was.'

(next page) Auditions: You can see nothing beyond the second row of blank stalls . . .

The Director

Touring companies have traditionally been run by actor-managers from the days when Shakespeare worked for the Burbages. Now it is the day of the director-manager. In most subsidised companies, from the National and the Royal Shakespeare to the large provincial repertories, directors are supreme.

Toby Robertson ultimately *is* the Prospect company. As its artistic director it is he who is finally responsible for the choice of plays (and of other directors to direct those he does not handle himself), for picking his ensemble of actors for the season, for deciding where and when to tour.

To make the programme work is the task of the general manager and his staff, and there is a board of directors overseeing the whole complex operation. But the success or failure of the year's work rests ultimately on the shoulders of the artistic director.

Inevitably he is something of an autocrat. Inevitably the company members have, as one actor put it, a love-hate relationship with him. It was always so, in the days of Irving or Kean or, at the Old Vic itself, Lilian Baylis or Tyrone Guthrie. The theatre does not work well as a democracy or under committee rule.

Toby Robertson has been running Prospect for twelve years and has nurtured it from being a summer-seasons-only company to the leading touring theatre in the country, with an international reputation.

The year which this book describes was a very exceptional one for Prospect. It was the year in which a marriage took place between Prospect as a company and the Old Vic theatre, with all its illustrious theatrical ghosts, to create Prospect At The Old Vic—a touring company with its own home theatre. For the first time in its life, the company did not have to break up at the end of each season. It became a continuous entity, playing from one year into the next.

Despite all these organisational distractions, the director's first priority is to get the plays on. This year five productions are being staged: *Hamlet* and *Antony And Cleopatra,* both directed by Toby Robertson himself, Shaw's *St. Joan* and Dryden's version of the Antony and Cleopatra story, *All for Love*. Besides these there is an experimental production, part dance, part drama, called *War Music,* based on part of Homer's *Iliad.*

The productions cover a spread of centuries and styles and not all, of course, attract full houses. Actors are cast for their suitability not for one part but for a 'line' of parts through the repertory. Timothy West, for example, plays Claudius in *Hamlet*, Enobarbus in *Antony* and the Narrator in *War Music*; Robert Eddison the Inquisitor in *St. Joan*, the Soothsayer in *Antony* and, later in the season, the Ghost in *Hamlet.*

Toby Robertson is directing *Hamlet* for the first time in his career. There is a saying that if a director and his Hamlet agree, the play can be rehearsed in three weeks. Which is what he has. How does he approach the task?

Robertson is notorious for his flexibility as a director – another way of putting that would be that he is ready to change his productions up to the last minute, that he is never satisfied with what he already has. And, unlike some classical directors, he is not much given to theorising about the play.

'I try to give the actors as much freedom to explore as possible,' he explains. 'We don't sit around talking about it. We do it. Some of the things that you plan in the study simply don't work on the stage. Other things can only be discovered when you are out there. We may spend all morning rehearsing a scene and still not have set it. And I don't mind a hoot if, after all that, the actors go and do it differently tomorrow. You are working with thirty people, all of whom have personalities which the director can feed off. I could say "Move here, do this, do that" and the actors would do it blindly, but they wouldn't have a reason for what they did.

'In the end I have a power of veto – it must not become direction by a committee. But I

Robin Archer (designer), Derek Jacobi and Toby Robertson with costume sketches for Hamlet

City Sugar

prefer not to have to use it. I try to set a pattern for them to work within. This is an actor's theatre.'

Rehearsals

(Rehearsals for *Hamlet* begin on a Monday morning in March.)

A typical rehearsal day begins at 9.00 a.m. with Toby Robertson, accompanied by Bach on a cassette in his office, dictating to his secretary the changes he made in the much-changed text at yesterday's rehearsal. Some lines were cut, some were restored. 'I do a rough-cut of the text before we start – obviously the four-hour Hamlet is not for us – but I make the final version in rehearsal.'

Shakespeare's text, as finally published in the Folio of 1623, was cut in performance. Two different Quarto versions exist, published in his own lifetime, giving a variety of cuts and the modern director has to pick and choose between the three versions. Typed and bound in the standard form used for film and theatre scripts, stapled into a soft brown cover, it might be a contemporary play – except that the cut-out title window on the front reads 'The Tragedy Of Hamlet Prince Of Denmark'.

The prompt copy – D.S.M.'s cues on left

On this particular morning, Toby Robertson has had about four hours sleep, after attending another Prospect opening, of *St. Joan* with a separate company, in Bath the night before. By 10 o'clock the actors are drifting in and assembling in the dressing room behind the stage where instant coffee is dispensed for a 50 pence contribution a week. By 10.30 everyone has climbed the endless backstage stairs to the rehearsal room at the top of the Old Vic for the morning movement class.

This is partly a keep-fit measure, partly a way of training the actors' bodies to move with elegance on the stage. Donald Fraser, the musical director, sits at an old upright piano in the corner while the movement director, William Louther, a former Martha Graham dancer, takes the class.

Derek Jacobi, Toby Robertson, Timothy West and John Nettleton (Polonius)

William Louther with dancers

The company sit cross-legged on the floor in bare feet, wearing headscarves and woolly caps, grasping their ankles, bobbing their foreheads to the ground, rolling their heads to the strains of a Beethoven sonata. It is obvious from their hollow backs which of them are trained dancers. But after a few mornings the class has helped give the company an identity. They have stretched and gasped for breath in unison and it binds them together.

On stage that morning, the scene being rehearsed is Laertes' leave-taking from Ophelia, with Polonius's long and familiar catalogue of advice – 'This above all, to thine own self be true' – followed by his interrogation of Ophelia about the advances Hamlet has been making. Until you have sat through a morning of it, you do not realise how many ways there are of playing a scene of no more than a hundred lines with just one table and a bench for props.

Most of the direction consists of asking questions. Is Polonius giving sincerely good advice or is he revealing the deviousness of his own character? How can you convey that he is not to be trusted and still allow him to get his laughs? How afraid is Ophelia of her father? When he pooh-poohs the possibility of Hamlet really loving her, does she obey him dutifully or resentfully? And anyway does she love Hamlet or not? And so on.

'Nuances, nuances,' says director Toby Robertson after three or four playings-through. 'Laertes has gone. The house isn't going to be the same.' He advances on Ophelia very menacingly with Polonius's line: 'What is between you? Give me up the truth!' and involuntarily Ophelia backs away. 'That's what I want,' he says, suddenly dropping into conversation again.

The two deputy stage managers sitting in the front stalls tell him it is 12.15 and there are extra dancers waiting to be auditioned. They have been making notes. Every time the scene is 'blocked' – tried out – the moves are notated on the prompt copy. The left-hand, blank pages of the script are pencilled in with a sketch of the stage furniture and a description of the moves made by each character on the stage. It is done in pencil because at the next run-through it may be different. The rubber is used more often than the pencil at this stage. While one DSM notes the blocking, the other is ready to prompt the actors – he is 'on the book'.

There is a system for writing down moves in a set of shorthand symbols. The stage is mentally divided into areas: up-stage (back) and down-stage (front), centre stage or left and right (stage left and stage right are the opposite of the audience's left and right). Each section can be described by initials, thus: 'u.c.l.' means 'up-stage centre left' and 'd.c.r.' means 'downstage centre right'. So the line:

Pol x d.c.r.

means that Polonius crosses to downstage centre right.

Left and right can also be written P and O-P, standing for 'Prompt' and 'Opposite-Prompt', because the prompt corner is traditionally stage-left.

Blocking is extremely tiring. They have changed the moves five times already. 'It drives you mad,' mutters Marje Williams, the DSM, rubbing it out all over again.

It is now 12.30 and there are four tin-lids spread along the front of the stage bulging with cigarette ends. Paper cups of cold coffee stand about on the edge of the stage and beside the front stalls. 'I think that's going to work frightfully well,' says the director, as they finally break off and Polonius lights his pipe for the umpteenth time and returns to being John Nettleton. Thank goodness it is Thursday and pay day.

In the course of the first week's rehearsal the position of 'To be or not to be' has been altered twice. It has been tried as a soliloquy right at the beginning of the first court scene, and has been delivered straight to Ophelia sitting at a table. The entrance of the players has been blown up into a big set piece of dancing and tumbling and then cut right down again because it was holding up the action.

The graveyard scene has also been played many ways. Instead of a trap-door the grave is to be a sarcophagus 'trucked' (wheeled) on for the scene. How is Laertes to drop Ophelia's body and jump out of it to grapple with Hamlet? The grave will have to have a carpet in it. Perhaps also a bag of potting compost for the grave-digger. How is the grave to be got rid of in time for the next scene?

Where should the interval be placed? During the week it is moved twice and ends up back where it was.

By the Saturday morning, Toby Robertson is ready to try a run-through – or 'stagger-through' as he puts it. Before it begins he stands on the bare stage, backed only by its stark brick wall, to address the cast sitting in the stalls. 'Give yourselves to your fellow-artists and something may happen. Leave it to me to say "That's working" or "That isn't". I want to see if we have a good skeleton there.'

So, without books or scenery or lighting, in jeans and T-shirts and bare feet, they try fitting together all the pieces they have been rehearsing separately. It takes three hours. At the end the director gives 'notes' – the first set of many to come.

He is quite tough with them: 'I do find too much of the Shakespearean voice and manner. You are doing it too heavy and pomposo. You are probably busy thinking of your lines and moves. But unless you play naturally, we lose the nastiness of that court at Elsinore. There really is rank corruption there. We want to shock them with its corruption and brutishness. It needs to be tougher, nastier, grasping, evil, coarse, ruthless and *hard*' – he is haranguing them, it is quite a speech.

Suzanne Bertish (Ophelia)

Then he relents somewhat: 'There are a lot of extremely good things – a lot of good relationships which I'll talk to you about separately. I don't want to give detailed notes now except, Gravedigger – I think you're only about 38, perhaps 40, not older. Horatio – just because you're not passion's slave I don't think you should become too melancholy. Everybody – now we must refine. There's a lot to do and only two weeks to do it in.'

The cast disperses into the Waterloo Road on a Saturday afternoon, which is most people's time off.

Decor

Long before rehearsals begin the director and the designer co-ordinate their intentions with the aid of a set model. Robin Archer, the designer of *Hamlet*, has created a single setting for the whole play out of ten vast, dusky drapes, dimly patterned in such a way that they could be exterior or interior castle walls.

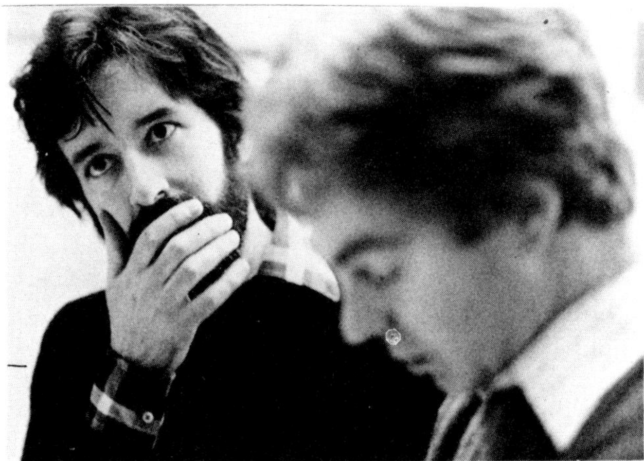

Robin Archer with Derek Jacobi

'The idea is to convey a feeling of claustrophobia, as though they will never open out into daylight. They are also easy to tour and to set up,' he explains. 'You can't afford to build an elaborate set and lose a day's performance putting it up every time you move.'

Trucking and rigging the set costs approximately £2,500 a time. Keith Edmundson, the technical manager, is responsible for getting the set to fit each theatre and to satisfy the stringent safety and fire regulations.

'Few people realise how much these add to the cost of set building, especially in London where they are fiercest,' he says. 'Everything forward of the safety curtain must be made of materials which are not only flame-proofed but will put themselves out.'

In practice this means using a material called 'silk noile' which costs £100 a sheet. All thin timber or plywood must be fireproofed, which doubles its cost.

Composer Donald Fraser

The claustrophobia of the sets is also the inspiration of the music which Donald Fraser is writing for *Hamlet*. It is a series of chilling and eerie sound effects.

For the opening tableau, for example, three discordant bell chimes strike together through the darkness. A strange chirruping heralds the imminent appearance of the ghost. A live trumpet with an echo, played in combination with a tape of the same music, gives the effect of fanfares bounding off the castle battlements into endless space.

'It's like composing a film score,' Donald Fraser explains. 'The music is there to focus the mood of the play at a particular moment.'

When you are touring continually with the minimum of set, the actors and their costumes *are* the scenery to an important extent. The designers' costume sketches are photographed and pasted into a large book – known in the wardrobe as the 'Bible'. Pinned alongside them are samples of the fabrics to be used. Often, for economy's sake, they are furnishing fabrics, which can save £1,000 a show.

'A lot of this is old rubbish,' says Robin Archer, supervising the fitting of the grandiose cloak of the First Player. 'This is all cheap curtaining that started off as bright orange or yellow lurex. We take it to someone and ask them to dye it a bad black. As a result it comes out reddish, greenish or goldish and looks old, rich and rather tasteful.' To enrich the effect, gold paint mixed with glue is applied with a

Painting the stagecloth for the floor (insert) the final effect

glue gun, as decoration.

You can achieve much with illusion but one thing which cannot be made out of cheap substitutes causes one of the heaviest wardrobe bills – boots and shoes. A pair of thigh boots costs £95 to make.

'Spear-carriers have to put up with what we've got left over from old productions,' says the wardrobe mistress, Vivienne Jenkins. 'We wouldn't put anyone in a pair that's too small. But we might put them in a pair that's too big and pad them out.'

The costumes are mostly made by outworkers who specialise in theatre clothing. Every theatre company has its circle of makers, and there are six of them working on costumes for *Hamlet*.

The definition of a prop is something that can be picked up and carried by the actor. The prop shop practises the same arts of disguise. Metal finishes are simulated with polyester resin. What look like bronze shields, helmets and sword belts turn out to be fibreglass and latex. And it is amazing what rich trimmings can be made out of webbing, piano felt, plastic pipe and piped glue, which looks like filigree cake icing.

Stage swords are liable to cost £80 each and are always getting notched and dented. Foils for duels tend to break near the points. Yorick's (fibreglass) skull has to be obtained from a medical model-makers for £25. A real one, alas poor skull, would be too fragile to stand up to nightly use.

(top) The wardrobe
(middle) A fitting for the First Player
(bottom) Beard and crown for Player King

The Actors

What does it feel like to play Hamlet? After a week Derek Jacobi is beginning to find out. It means three hours on the stage, almost uninterrupted, during which every eye must be on you.

From his first bitter jibe at the King – 'A little more than kin and less than kind' – until his last gasp – 'The rest is silence' – lies a Grand National course for an actor. It stretches for over 1,100 lines, full of pitfalls and peaks, soliloquies and climaxes in which he must act madness, real or feigned, dissemble with Claudius, tease Polonius, be ruthless with Rosencrantz and Guildenstern, break Ophelia's heart, be heartbroken by his mother and then, having put everything into this, fight an elaborate and exhausting duel before dying. Many seasoned actors have been winded before the closet scene with the Queen, let alone the duel.

Derek Jacobi amazed the rest of the cast by arriving at the first rehearsal word perfect. 'Usually I learn my lines along with the moves when the play is being blocked, but this part is so long that I didn't want to waste rehearsal time. I decided to get the lines out of the way first if I could. I was pleased to find how well they'd stuck.'

Jacobi is well aware of the steepness of the mountain he has set himself to climb. 'Unless you learn to pace it, it's the most knackering show ever. You must discover how much energy you need to use in each particular scene so that you don't exhaust yourself too soon. Health is terribly important to an actor. I keep a rowing machine at home to help keep me fit.

'As an actor you need three things – energy and luck and talent. You may have all the talent necessary but you still have to have the luck to be given the chances and then, when you get the chances, you must have the energy to take them. Of course, once you're on, the stage produces its own energy. You may arrive at the theatre sometimes feeling, "God, how am I going to do it?" but when you get out there, the energy comes out of the air like an electric charge. It's a physical feeling. There are times when the audience somehow lets you know that you are hitting it properly, when you know what is coming is going to go right.'

Luck has played a considerable part in Derek Jacobi's unconventional career – he never went to drama school. 'I had three major lucky breaks. At Cambridge I did a production of *Edward II*, directed by Toby Robertson, which we played in the Memorial Gardens at Stratford. A director of Birmingham Rep saw it and he remembered me when I wrote round later trying to get a job. At Birmingham I got three plum parts and, by luck, I was seen in them by Laurence Olivier and he invited me to join him at Chichester in what was to become the National Theatre company. The third piece of luck came there. I was understudying Jeremy Brett. He was bought out to play in a film and I got his parts – including Laertes in the opening *Hamlet*.'

When the television series, *I, Claudius,* catapulted Jacobi to fame he had already worked hard for 15 years on the classical stage. 'It made me known to a vast audience who had never heard of me. I used to get letters asking if I had ever acted before.'

In fact he had agreed to do Hamlet with Prospect before the television serial came up. Why? 'Everyone who aspires to be a classical actor has a Hamlet somewhere inside him. It's become a sort of examination hoop to jump through. You can do all sorts of classical parts but this one is the test. People say, "Yes, but what is his Hamlet like?" I hope I play it more than once because there's no end to it. You keep changing all the time as you find your rhythm.'

Even after he had been playing the part for months he found it always gave him nerves. 'You think this is the night they'll find you out. You have to prove your ability each time you do it. I can't, for example, have a glass of wine at lunchtime or go to the pictures in the afternoon if I am playing Hamlet that night. It looms up from about two o'clock onwards as

Derek Jacobi with Timothy West – 15 minutes to go

the focal point of the day. You spend almost all day thinking about it.'

What is it like, at the other end of the scale, to be a walk-on?

Jeffrey Daunton, who is 28, is one of these although he has a great deal more to do than just walk on to the stage carrying a spear. He is hectically busy changing costumes and listening for cues throughout the performance because he 'doubles' in five parts. They include Francisco, Reynaldo and Cornelius, though few people in the audience know them by name or realise it is the same actor playing them. The other two parts are as soldiers in opposing armies (a quick change of cloaks and helmets there).

Jeffrey has less than 30 lines to speak all evening – though plenty of people wait a long time to have that many – so what makes him want to do it?

'Burton and all that lot started by carrying spears,' he justifiably points out. 'The experience you get in a company like this is really good. You are learning to carry your costumes and your wigs, you are learning to vary your make-up, you can observe really top actors at work, you are learning your craft. The money's not that fantastic but what's money?'

Jeffrey has been trying for two years to get into Prospect. This year he is rewarded for patience by getting an audition and a total of

Walk-ons' dressing room

nine parts in the season.

'I got interested at my comprehensive school, which had a good drama section. I was advised either to go to drama school or become an ASM straight away. I went to Guildford as an ASM and got my Equity card. Eventually I went to drama school for three years, came out and went touring with Brian Rix and his company.

'Last year I was out of work almost all the year, with a few days' work doing television, a commercial and a film to keep me going – just. Luckily I could live at home. After that, this job is welcome and there's the attraction of touring and going abroad to places you would probably never visit otherwise.'

Touring is expensive for the actor, despite the touring allowance of £35 a week. This only just covers digs, meals and necessities. 'You can soon be out of pocket on drinks, eating out and having a taxi home at night,' says Jeffrey Daunton.

Older actors with families are much less inclined to tour for long. 'I missed having a summer holiday with my kids for three out of the last four years,' says one of them who turned down this summer's tour.

Most of them reckon that it is a reasonable average to be in work for a third of the year. If they stay at home that will be in television or films more often than not, and will earn them at least as much money as solid weeks of touring. When they join Prospect it is for the sake of the work, not the money.

There are no fortunes paid in a company like this, though you often work a 13-hour day for six days a week. There are three salary brackets. No actor gets less than £60 a week (the Equity minimum for touring at this time was £38.50). Walk-ons and bit parts are worth from £60 to £75, according to ability and experience. The middle range of parts brings in around £100 a week.

"Goodnight, sweet prince"

None of the principals, who might well earn as much as £500 from a commercial West End management, gets more than £150 a week. Since touring rules out the possibility of extra daytime engagements in television or films, their financial sacrifice to play in the classics is considerable.

Finance

How does a classical repertory company pay its way? The short answer is that it can't be done, certainly not these days if it ever could. Not because there are not enough people who want to see the classics – in the course of the year approximately 200,000 people at home and abroad saw the company's five productions. But the classics are frighteningly expensive to stage.

The production of *Hamlet* required a company of 43 on the road. The sets, even when kept to a minimum, are large and costly – *Hamlet's* cost £10,000. The costumes, though heavily pruned, cost even more than the budgeted £15,000. Stage furniture and props accounted for about £3,000 more. The final cost of production was £36,000, which was several thousands more than planned.

What is worse is that a company has to spend this many times over to provide the variety of a repertoire. Five productions on this scale eat up £180,000 in a year, all of that visible on the stage. The invisible costs – of administration, transport, travel, publicity, touring allowances, national insurance, accountancy and other overheads – double that figure.

The cost of a year's work on the road and in a London theatre was £360,000. And each year it costs more to do the same thing.

The company's income is a combination of box office takings and subsidy. The Arts Council subsidizes its touring in the United Kingdom on the basis that each week in a provincial theatre runs at a loss. In this particular year the subsidy amounted to £240,000. The Edinburgh Festival offered a fee of £45,000 for a three-week engagement. The British Council bears the cost of touring abroad and the company makes a small profit, £3,000, on its management fee. Commercial sponsorship by W. D. and H. O. Wills helped guarantee the company against loss in its London season.

The rest of the cost has to be covered by box office takings on tour and at the Old Vic. The maximum possible 'take' at the Old Vic (which seats only 878) at current seat prices was £2,000 a performance, or £14,000 a week. But in practice this is a figure that cannot be realised.

In any 'full house' there are bound to be ticket agency and party bookings at a discount. There is always a small number of complimentary seats. Although 100 per cent of the seats may have bottoms on them, the theatre will not receive 100 per cent of the money: 70 per cent is a reasonable figure to average, 80 per cent is very good, 90 per cent fantastic.

It the company had played only its most popular productions, notably *Hamlet*, it could have run at a profit in the short term but it would not have been doing its job. In the end it had a deficit over the year of approximately £40,000. Such are the costs of touring and presenting classics which no commercial management would touch.

Lady-in-waiting waiting

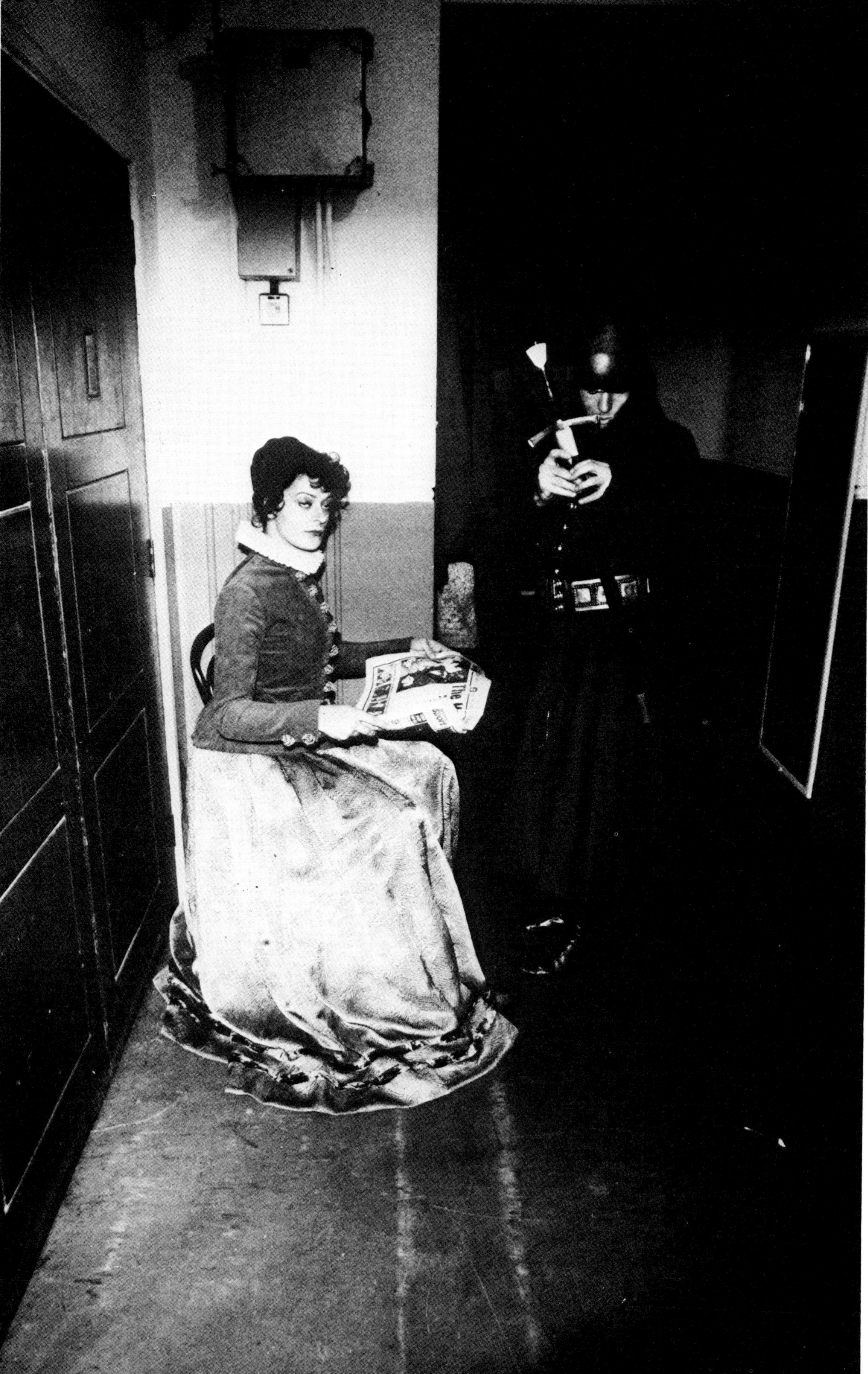
The

Out of Town

(In April *Hamlet* opened its out-of-town, pre-London tour at the New Theatre, Oxford.)

Getting-In

No one on the production staff of a touring company ever has a free Sunday. Sunday is the day of the 'get-in' – the theatrical word for moving house. The scenery has to be set on a strange stage, the costumes and wigs set out in strange dressing rooms, the lighting rigged and pre-set – all of which takes the best part of the day, apart from travelling time.

The costumes arrive hanging in eight box-shaped wardrobes, gaily painted with stripes or clouds or animals. Inevitably they are never quite ready. The wardrobe mistress and her assistants immediately set about sewing, or dyeing, or repairing them further. Some are being sprayed with aerosols of grey paint to age them.

One still has to be made – for the English Ambassador, a role that was cut early in rehearsal and only restored at the last moment. 'I've told them he can't be put back till his frock's ready,' says a harrowed wardrobe mistress. To the wardrobe, all costumes, male as well as female, are 'frocks'.

One of the scenery drapes has been left behind in London by mistake and someone has been told to bring it. The props travel in skips and are being set out in the dressing rooms or on tables behind the stage, one left and one right, according to the entrance at which they will be needed.

Every theatre raises different problems. The New Theatre, Oxford, has what is called a 'bastard prompt corner' – that is, it is stage right instead of the usual stage left. The deputy stage manager, who is going to operate it, has to discover how much, or rather how little, of the action can be seen from there, besides mastering all the switches which confront one like a pilot's panel. While operating the cue lights, the DSM is also following 'the book' – the acting text as finally amended – to prompt any actor who 'dries'.

It is early on Monday morning, the day of the technical and dress rehearsals. Most in evidence are four deputy or assistant stage managers – Marje, who will 'run the corner', Garth, who operates the music and sound effects, Ted, who supervises the setting and striking (taking on and off) of stage furniture from scene to scene, and Lance, who is responsible for sending everyone on with the correct props – be it a dagger or crown they should be wearing, a scroll or goblet they should be carrying, or Yorick's skull which must be hidden inside the grave convenient to hand for the gravedigger to unearth. The better the actor, the better he is at remembering his own props – but they must always be checked.

One of the less enviable tasks of the stage

management, usually the junior ASM, is to set off the maroons. A maroon, which is the size of a large cotton reel, is really a highly-compressed firework, which has to be set off well away from the stage to provide the effect of cannon. The rules stipulate it must be inside a welded tank. 'Right! Loud Bang! Everybody ready for a loud bang!' People affect nonchalance and go on climbing ladders or hammering nails but the test explosion, when it comes, makes everybody jump.

Meanwhile, on hands and knees, people are marking the positions of the corners of the throne, the council table, the Queen's bed, Ophelia's tomb, with pieces of coloured sticky tape – red for this scene, yellow for that, blue for another. Small as they are, they have to be found in a hurry in the dark or an actor may have his moves and his concentration ruined by finding that a table or a chair is a couple of feet out of position.

Another stagehand is moving about the stage being 'lit' in the positions that will be occupied by the actors. Every theatre's lighting board varies and the touring company brings and rigs extra lamps of its own. The theatres they play provide their own chief electrician, master carpenter, dressers and housekeeper.

The company manager is responsible for the delicate exercise of allocating dressing rooms.

'You learn,' says Clare Fox, 'by bitter experience who can't stand whom.' Only the two, or perhaps three or four, principals get a dressing room to themselves. Tradition has it that the more junior the actor, the farther his dressing room is away from the stage.

The walk-ons, like the wardrobe, are always at the very top of the steep backstage stairs, which makes little sense in Shakespeare when most of them are continually changing their costumes and their parts as members of the stage army. In the course of the evening a junior will walk on in perhaps six different guises as soldier, courtier or servant, with no time to hare up and down three flights of stairs between each change. Many of them have to use quick-change areas just behind the wings, dressing directly out of the travelling wardrobe boxes.

Clare describes her role as company manager as 'a glorified nanny – if anything goes wrong it's my fault.' She it is who finds digs and doctors, copes with private crises or bad news from home, smooths hurt feelings and, most important, produces the pay packets every Thursday. They are ordinary buff pay packets with hard cash inside and the actors' names outside, even those of the stars. Actors on tour need the money in the hand. Prudently she sees that the money is well concealed about her and handed over at varying times and places. 'You wouldn't guess I was carrying £8,000, would you?'

In England the cast are left to find their own accommodation. Many have their favourite places from previous visits, though the reliable old theatrical digs run by theatrical landladies are disappearing now, because touring is on so much smaller a scale. 'We've got everything this week from the grandest hotel to the cheapest digs – no baths after 9.30 p.m. Someone's staying on a houseboat.'

Everyone is required to write his address on the noticeboard inside the stage door. It is chock-a-block with lists. Call sheets, dressing room details, good-luck telegrams to the company in general from well-wishers and from the leading actor, Derek Jacobi, all compete for space and drawing pins; and somewhere, hanging on forlornly dog-eared and pin-holed, is the invitation from the local padre representing the Actors' Church Union.

Over in the prompt corner, Marje, the DSM, is sorting out the cue board. There are rows of button switches operating cue lights –

Clare Fox – pay day

D.S.M. Marje Williams

red for 'Stand by', green for 'Go', some of them irrelevantly labelled 'Orchestra', 'Projector', 'Limes' or 'OP Trap'. These are being altered with sticky tape to 'Musicians' (backstage, not in the pit), 'Maroons', 'Electrics', 'Flies' or 'House-lights'. Beside the cue board hangs the house telephone by which she can get through to the front of house, the lighting console, the stage door and so forth. In front of it is the microphone through which she can address the cast via the inter-com.

Marje is in a bit of a spin because at the last minute the interval has been moved. All those cues written in the prompt book need altering for several pages to take account of it. 'And to think I turned down a nice, simple show because I thought this would be more interesting.'

It is, of course, more interesting. But at a moment like this, with only one rehearsal to finalise everything – they have just decided to combine the technical and the dress rehearsals for lack of time – the responsibilities for getting everything right in that prompt corner are fairly frightening.

During the morning the actors have been arriving, by rail or road, and drifting in to look at the stage and get the feel of this unfamiliar instrument which they will have to play. The rehearsal is called for one o'clock and starts 50 minutes late because a new lighting plot for the play's opening has to be tried out.

Much of an actor's life is spent waiting. While they wait, they lurch about under the unfamiliar restriction of cloaks and boots, helmets and crowns. What seemed nimble moves in rehearsal now seem impossibly slow and ponderous.

The actors feel and look like strangers. One spear-carrier misses an entrance completely because he has gone back to the dressing room. Another finds himself on stage at the wrong moment altogether. 'We don't usually have the pleasure of seeing you in this scene,' remarks Claudius with gentle irony. '*Wear* the costumes, don't let them imprison you!' calls the director's voice from the darkened auditorium.

It is 6 o'clock before they break for drinks and sandwiches, brought in from the pub next door. Further difficulties arise in the second half. The Queen's bed sounds like a state coach as it is trundled on for the closet scene – 'For God's sake pick it up and carry it!' – while the Queen's long velvet train is coming away and has to be sewn back on to her.

Behind the arras a DSM crouches holding a block of polystyrene for Hamlet to plunge his sword into, in place of Polonius. The trouble is, it squeaks when the sword goes in. 'So would you,' says the DSM testily. 'We'll try foam rubber.'

After eight hours on your feet, most of them waiting, it is hard to love the director, the play or the author, who seems to have contrived so many difficulties in staging. By the final court scene, tempers are short. They break at five past ten, just soon enough to get out of costume and into the pub for the last quarter of an hour's drinking time. They need it.

First night

The first night at Oxford begins casually enough, an hour before curtain up, with two stage hands sweeping the stage. Clouds of dust are rising in the patch of light that surrounds Hamlet and Laertes, who are rehearsing the duel under the critical eye of the fight director, Ian Mackay. To one's surprise he is small and bird-like, one of the highly select company of fencing masters who arrange fights for the major companies.

However often it has been practised – and they have been practising every day for a month – the duel has to be rehearsed before every performance for safety reasons. Hamlet, after three hours on stage, is bound to be tiring. Any uncertainty can mean injury.

Mackay varies each duel according to the fencing abilities of the actors ('These two are very good'). There are 72 moves in all, with cup-hilted rapier and dagger. They are divided into three sequences by the dialogue. The whole fight lasts over two minutes. Each lunge and answering parry is written down in a ballet-like notation with tiny drawings and the name of each position written beneath. It is as easy to 'dry' in a duel as it is in a speech. 'The most important thing is to keep eye contact,' explains Mackay, 'so that if that happens, the other actor can see it and both go into the "escape routine". You bring both weapons down, close together, and go back to the beginning of the sequence.'

Apart from practising the fight, Derek Jacobi has been in his dressing room since 5.30 – two hours before the show will 'go up'. He hasn't slept for two nights and this afternoon there was a drill going outside his hotel. 'I spend the night with the show going round and round in my head – entrances, exits, cuts. I'm not able to eat yet. I'm living on Dextrosol. I feel desperately tired but when you get out there, you somehow find the energy. There must be a way of doing it without flogging yourself to death, and I've got to find it. And yet, if you don't go flat out, you're not giving 100 per cent of your performance.'

To add to his worries, he has had an unspecified throat infection that has baffled the doctors all through rehearsals. Glasses of water are set

Hamlet and Laertes rehearsing the duel

out for him at strategic places in the wings. It is all that can be done.

The 'half' is called over the backstage tannoy – 'Half an hour, please, ladies and gentlemen' – followed, much too soon it seems, by the 'quarter'. Wigs, newly dressed, are fitted by the wigmaster, Robert Gardner. Hamlet has grown his own hair, beard and moustache. A wig would be impossibly hot and sweaty in such an active part. Invitations are issued to a wine-and-cheese cast party afterwards. The trumpeter can be heard warming up. People, as usual, are borrowing make-up from one another. (It is not all Leichner – a lot of young actors save money by going to the Boots make-up counter.)

'Five minutes, please,' says the sepulchral voice over the dressing-room loudspeakers and behind it can now be heard the subdued, bubbling sound of an assembling audience, like the breaking of a distant sea. Each actor feels at this moment nakedly exposed and vulnerable. They have their own ways of exorcising their fears. Superstition runs deep, as it does in any risky profession – motor racing, bull fighting, gambling. Actors put charms on their dressing tables.

Timothy West sets out a collection of glass animals. 'One day I found I'd forgotten them and then I realised how much they meant to me.' Barbara Jefford keeps a special stone, the colour of a conker. 'My husband (John Turner) gave it to me and I would feel very odd without it.' On Derek Jacobi's table the pots and sticks and liners are marshalled fastidiously like troops on a parade ground. The telegrams and good luck cards are lined up on the wall with impeccable dressing.

By such rituals actors try to contain their fear of the many-headed beast waiting out there for them in the dark. They are as superstitious of bad luck omens as sailors. Hence the taboos against whistling in the dressing room, or naming that unluckiest of plays, *Macbeth* – often referred to, for safety, as 'the Scottish play'.

'Beginners, please,' murmur the loudspeakers. Most of the beginners (it means those on first, not those who are inexperienced) are already pacing the wings in a state either of friendliness or withdrawal. Distantly one can hear the front of house announcement: 'Ladies and gentlemen, will you kindly take your seats? The curtain will rise in one minute.' The phrase lingers although there is no curtain down, as is increasingly the custom with Shakespeare productions.

There is much throat clearing in the passages and the occasional 'Good luck' and 'Merde'. Why the French word? It is like spitting for luck – but why in French no one is sure. 'Stand by, please,' murmurs Marje in a super-cool voice into her microphone in the prompt corner, with a finger poised to take down the house lights.

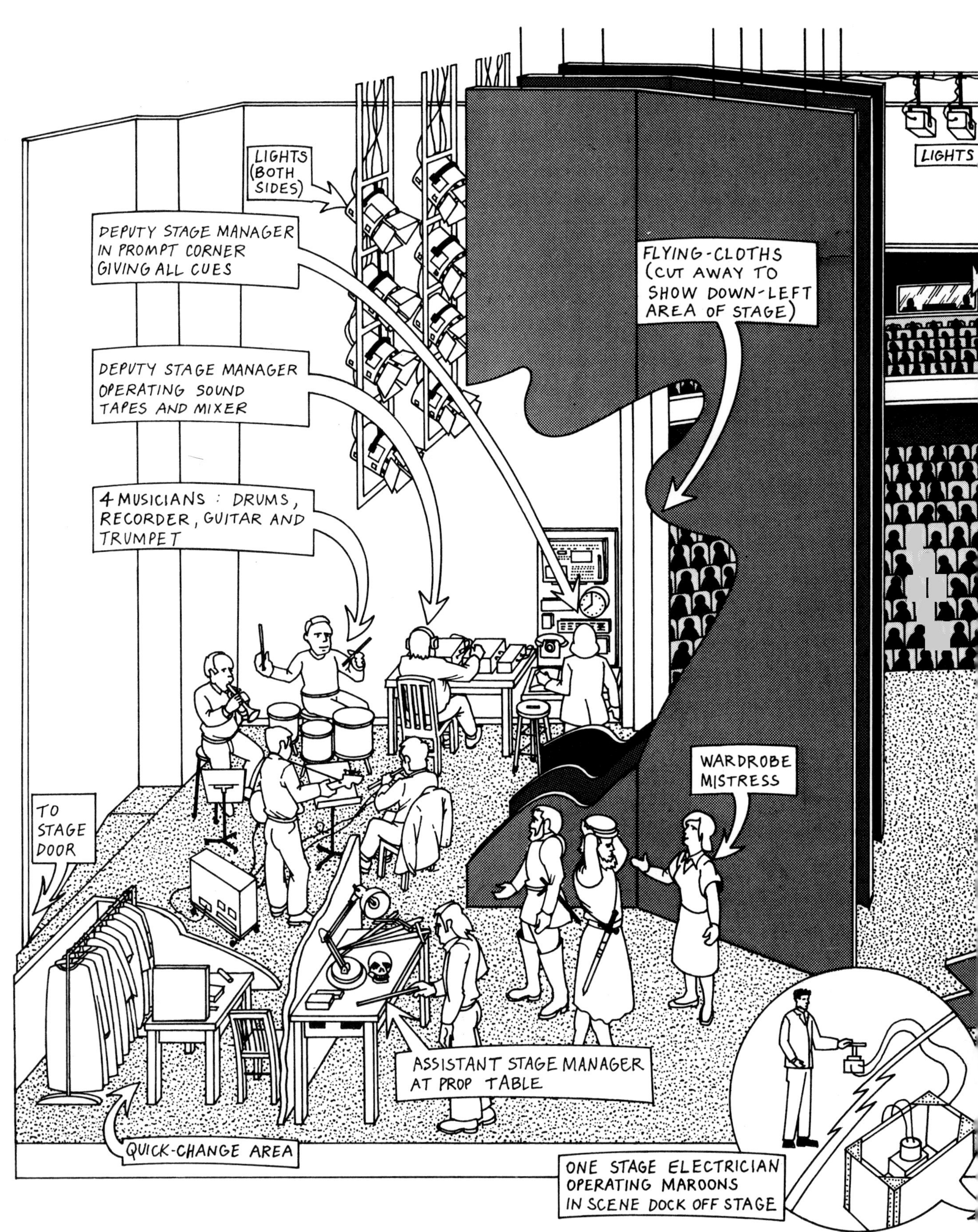
LIGHTS (BOTH SIDES)
LIGHTS
DEPUTY STAGE MANAGER IN PROMPT CORNER GIVING ALL CUES
FLYING-CLOTHS (CUT AWAY TO SHOW DOWN-LEFT AREA OF STAGE)
DEPUTY STAGE MANAGER OPERATING SOUND TAPES AND MIXER
4 MUSICIANS : DRUMS, RECORDER, GUITAR AND TRUMPET
WARDROBE MISTRESS
TO STAGE DOOR
ASSISTANT STAGE MANAGER AT PROP TABLE
QUICK-CHANGE AREA
ONE STAGE ELECTRICIAN OPERATING MAROONS IN SCENE DOCK OFF STAGE

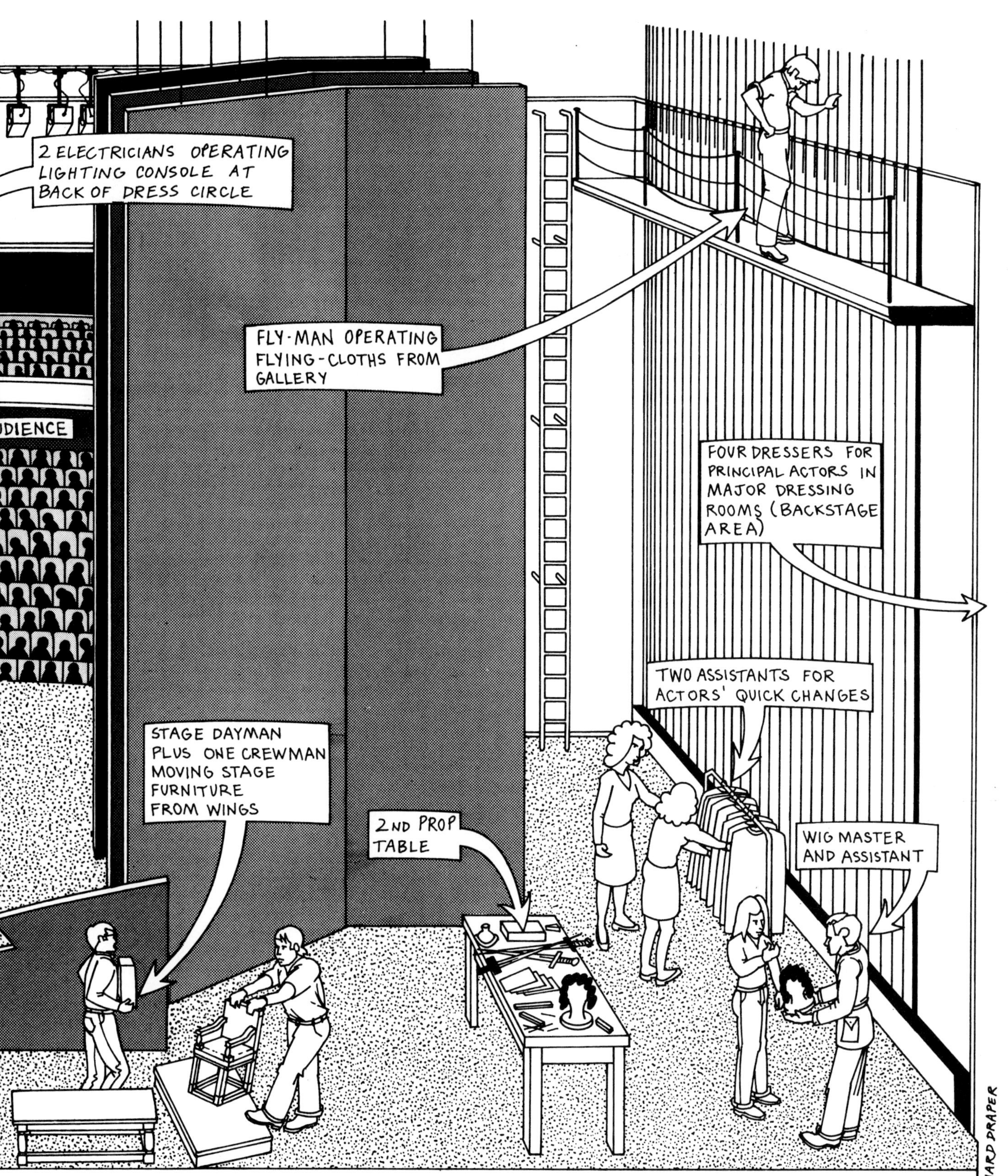
2 ELECTRICIANS OPERATING LIGHTING CONSOLE AT BACK OF DRESS CIRCLE
FLY-MAN OPERATING FLYING-CLOTHS FROM GALLERY
UDIENCE
FOUR DRESSERS FOR PRINCIPAL ACTORS IN MAJOR DRESSING ROOMS (BACKSTAGE AREA)
TWO ASSISTANTS FOR ACTORS' QUICK CHANGES
STAGE DAYMAN PLUS ONE CREWMAN MOVING STAGE FURNITURE FROM WINGS
2ND PROP TABLE
WIG MASTER AND ASSISTANT
RICHARD DRAPER

As they fade to darkness, a spotlight hits the front of the stage; the first eerie chord is struck by the musicians and the heads of the audience come into view, like rows of cobblestones lit by moonlight. Smoke billows from a smoke canister; the waiting guards grasp their pikes and thrust forward into the smoky space to turn it into the battlements of Elsinore, and suddenly the play is *on*.

'Stand by all those concerned in the first court scene . . .' The guards come off in a swish of greatcoats and wait behind the side drapes for their next entrance. Soon Polonius can be heard through the tinny loudspeaker in Claudius's dressing room, giving Laertes that endless good advice, while Claudius sits studying his next scene. Soon Hamlet is off doing a quick change in the adjoining dressing room. 'Did that sound all right to you?' 'Sounded fine but I jumped a cue.'

John Nettleton (Polonius)

The musicians in their dark backstage corner are screwing up their eyes over their paperbacks. The trumpeter hastily puts down a Michael Innes detective story just in time to sound the King's rouse. The stage rocks as a maroon explodes in its tank.

At last the interval. Polonius gratefully lights the pipe he has been concealing in his chamberlain's robes, saying between puffs to Rosencrantz and Guildenstern, 'I brought you on a bit early, I cut a great chunk of the fishmonger scene – apologies!' The director's voice can be heard going from dressing room to dressing room: 'Angel . . . wonderful . . . absolutely right . . .' It may sound gushing, but amid the tension it is badly needed reassurance.

Up many flights of stairs, round many corners, in the walk-ons' shared dressing rooms, people do not call with reassuring remarks. 'Last night it was all jokes in here – tonight feels chilly by comparison, like a second night.' 'What do I do to make myself look very old, which I can take off again immediately afterwards?' 'Try white or ivory on the bridge of your nose.' There is no loudspeaker up here and the first vibrating chord of the second half takes them by surprise. 'Oh God . . .' a strolling player goes careering down the stairs to Elsinore, clutching his red wig.

So it goes by – 'To be or not to be', the nunnery scene, the play scene, the closet scene – Polonius is killed without a squeak, thanks to the foam rubber. Hamlet comes off panting after his chase and arrest, pulling off his coat and boots, mopping at the sweat, chucking the fifth soaking sweatshirt of the evening on to the pile on the dressing room radiator. He has 15 minutes, the only break of the night, in which to get his breath back for the final assault leading up to the duel. Shakespeare knew what he was doing when he arranged this rest for his leading actor. Without it, no one could play Hamlet. Derek Jacobi lights a cigarette – but there isn't time to finish it.

In the wings, Laertes is flexing his knees and his sword arm, loosening up for the duel. When it comes, they give it real venom, overturning chairs, leaping tables like the freshest of musketeers. As the four captains bear Hamlet from the stage, the maroons boom out again – only two out of three because the first explosions blew the detonator off the next. Finally, the curtain calls.

As they come off from the first call, the actors surreptitiously kick or fling off-stage the foils, the poisoned cup, bits of overturned furniture which are in the way. The noise of the audience is like the sea – a roaring, but not a menacing, breaking of waves, with 'Bravos' sounding in the foam as Hamlet steps forward for his own call.

At 10.40 the stage lights go down for the last time and the house lights come up. The director can be heard booming his 'Well dones'. The musicians are already in the pub next door where there were eight pints waiting on the bar at 10.45 precisely. Musicians have these matters well organised.

To an onlooker who has watched the fraught moments, the last-minute changes, the eleventh-hour licks of paint, the wonder is that everything is, somehow, just ready. 'It will be all right on the night' is a dangerously optimistic saying but the knowledge that there is no more time left does concentrate the mind, sharpen the reactions and bring forth wonders of improvisation.

At the cast party, Marje Williams, whose performance in the prompt corner is as vital as that of any leading actor, was able to relax for the first time since stage rehearsals began. 'I admit I get a bang from the actual performance and the concentration it demands. I put up with the misery of the rest of it for that.'

On this particular night, the most testing moment came when the light on the prompt corner telephone started flashing in the middle of a complicated sequence of music and lighting cues. It could have meant any emergency – a fire backstage, an actor struck down or missing, an electrical breakdown . . . When Marje picked it up a strange voice said: 'Is that you, Reg? Oh, wrong number.'

Afterwards such stories are passed from mouth to mouth as part of the unwinding process. In the late-night restaurant towards midnight, Hamlet, Claudius and others are sitting around, relieved by the reception but still wondering how it really went – perhaps a little afraid to ask the director when he joins them. Besides, everyone is too tired to go into it.

'It's lovely when it stops,' says Derek Jacobi, staring without interest at his plate. He can still scarcely eat. He leaves early to see if at last he can sleep. 'Good night, sweet prince,' says someone inevitably.

Timothy West (Claudius), Barbara Jefford (Gertrude)

At the Old Vic

Publicity

No company likes to risk opening a play 'cold' in London. An out-of-town tour is a chance to iron out staging problems – one of them, the trucking on stage of the Queen's noisy bed, was solved by dispensing with it altogether. By the time *Hamlet* returns to its home, the Old Vic, it has spent five weeks on the road, including a gruelling fortnight of one-night stands in Germany with hundreds of miles of coach travel every day.

Now, back on a familiar stage, the actors should be able to concentrate entirely on their performances and characterisation. They must be at their best because future 'business' depends on how critics and audiences react to the first week of performances.

Hamlet, untypically, opened sold out for three weeks, with an 'advance' of £21,000 already in the box office, thanks to the television reputations of Derek Jacobi and Timothy West. Even the previews were sold out. It is the custom to invite to these the managers of ticket agencies, large and small, and (shrewdly) the hall porters of major London tourist hotels. It may all help to build the 'word of mouth', that mysterious factor of personal recommendation which can sometimes save a show even after the newspaper critics have panned or roasted it as a 'turkey' or a 'bomber' – there are many synonyms for a flop but they are no comfort if you are in one.

Before opening night the publicity office (in this case one hard-worked girl) goes into high gear in attempting to build an audience. There are two press nights. The national newspapers' drama critics and show business correspondents, international papers, Reuters, BBC radio, certain prestigious weekly magazines – these are on the first night list. The majority of magazines, local papers, and tourist 'What's On' publications are invited to the second night.

Personal contacts are made to set up interviews with the leading actors (sometimes even the author) on radio and television, or with profile writers, show business and gossip columnists. There is a photocall at which the company in full costume perform the difficult feat, at 11 o'clock in the morning, of throwing themselves into excerpts from the play and freezing at dramatic moments for a row of blasé photographers. Production stills by the company's own photographer are given away. The rest of them are already up on the boards outside the theatre, soon to be joined, it is hoped, by favourable excerpts from the critics' notices. Handbills go out to the ticket agencies and social clubs; coach tour operators are offered reduced ticket prices for party bookings; the educational authority and school drama advisers are encouraged to arrange school visits (*Hamlet* is always on someone's examination syllabus).

Perhaps the biggest factor for success or failure is the ticket agencies, known as 'the Libraries'. If interested, they take half the seats in the house, usually the left hand side of the auditorium, while the theatre box office retains the right hand side. On a typical show, a third of the seats booked in advance will be sold by the libraries, a third by the box office and the remainder will be sold on the doors on the day of performance.

The first night audience for an unknown play would often be depressingly thin were it not for the giving of complimentary tickets – 'papering the house'. Obviously there are 'comps' for the management's friends, the 'angels' who have put up a share of the production costs (in a commercial theatre), the agents, relatives and friends of the cast (who may get four free seats each allocated to them). But in this case tickets are like gold dust.

Critics

The critics are greeted in the foyer by the theatre publicist, Priscilla Yates, given a programme and invited to have a drink in a private bar upstairs in the interval.

First nights generally 'go up' at 7 p.m., half an hour early, because morning newspaper deadlines vary from 10.45 p.m. to midnight. Even a speedy *Hamlet* plays for over three hours – overnight critics can scarcely ever see the duel – and will 'come down' about 10.15. No wonder critics do not often stay to applaud. If you see a man in an aisle seat, striding out and grabbing his coat, apparently unmoved during an ovation for the cast, he is not expressing displeasure, he is just a critic.

It is commonly, and wrongly, believed that critics decide together in the interval whether to turn their thumbs up or down on a show, like the Vestal Virgins at a gladiator contest. This persists in spite of the fact that their notices so often disagree. In fact there is a strong convention among critics that it is ungentlemanly and never done to speak to one another about that night's production.

Though actors owe much to the appreciation of critics – no one ever complained of a good notice – the two species are natural enemies. It is rare, and unwise, for them to be friends off-stage. Adverse criticism is always hard to forgive. It is harder still to believe it just, not because actors are so vain but because they are so vulnerable.

In another two hours the critics will be in their seats and the die will be cast. How does a director feel at this eleventh hour? 'I feel it belongs to the actors now,' Toby Robertson confesses privately. 'There are things which will never be quite as I want them. But you have to work with your actors and, especially, with your Hamlet. This Hamlet is perhaps a more rational man than I saw originally, but Derek has to find his own interpretation.'

In a radio interview that day, Derek Jacobi has been saying exactly that: 'In the end you can only say that's how *I* play Hamlet.' But he adds that his performance is more aggressive because of his director.

Both of them are showing the strain in the form of imaginary ailments, inability to eat and sleep, mysterious pains. 'My body is saying it doesn't want to do it,' says Jacobi.

The notices were, as usual, 'mixed'. You never get unmitigated compliments, let alone raves, for *Hamlet* because it is too rich a play, too much a Himalayan peak of a part, for anyone to give the definitive interpretation.

If Hamlet is a man of action, he will be criticised for not being a philosopher. He will either be not mad enough, or not sane enough, and so on. Unorthodox touches – such as this production's delivery of 'To be or not to be' not as a soliloquy but as an intimate confidence to Ophelia – will be praised by some and taken severely to task by others as 'not what Shakespeare intended' – as though Shakespeare had left explicit instructions.

Do actors read their notices? Leading actors always *say* they don't – and there are good reasons not to. 'But I heard enough about them to upset me,' said Derek Jacobi, some months later. 'If people come up and tell you not to take any notice of what X or Y said, you know they've given you a roasting. The one I did read insisted that I had got the stresses wrong in certain lines and suggested it was because I did not know what the lines meant. That was really a bit much, a bit insulting. It bothers you the next night when you play the lines. You assume, quite wrongly, that everyone there has read the notice too, and is thinking the same thing. The only thing to do as an actor is to forget it.' He obviously hadn't. It still rankled.

Even compliments can be unsettling because they can make the actor self-conscious the next time he plays it. 'A lot of effects are unconscious on the actor's part. You literally don't know how you get them. You come to that place again and you wonder what you did that made them say it was so good. Then you can easily be lost.'

Overseas

Repertory, tough and demanding as it is, gives you no time to recuperate. Fresh or tired, elated or downcast by the first night reception, the very next morning the cast starts work on a new play – *Antony and Cleopatra* – soon joined by Dryden's version of the same story, *All For Love.*

The strain of playing one Shakespeare play at night after rehearsing another all day is considerable. Altogether, there are four plays in production, all of them having to be ready within five weeks of one another. There is not quite enough energy left to work 13 hours a day, and there is a spate of resignations (mostly withdrawn later) among the overworked production staff.

No one has had a day off, other than Sundays, from March to July. The new productions are not played in to anyone's satisfaction. Some people are feeling the effects of cholera and typhoid injections in preparation for the five-week Middle Eastern tour which follows. Morale, for a few dangerous weeks, is floundering.

It is in this overstrained and overtired state that the company has to prepare to take *Antony and Cleopatra* as well as *Hamlet* on a tour of the Eastern Mediterranean. The British Council, showing the flag culturally at foreign festivals, fixes and pays for the extremely expensive travel involved, which no company could afford out of its own coffers.

From the company's point of view, foreign touring keeps the actors employed for so many weeks of the year, when it might otherwise have to disband for lack of enough touring dates at home. From the fees paid by foreign festival organisers there may be a modest profit of around £5,000. From the actors' point of view there is the attraction of a bit of relaxation in usually agreeable surroundings. They are put up at very good hotels and given a daily allowance of £8–£10 in local currency for meals.

A British Council representative gives a preliminary talk on their role as unofficial ambassadors and recommends prudent behaviour, salt tablets, and the removal of Marks and Spencer labels from their underwear before entering an Arab country. Only the barest of scenery is taken on tour, and two lorries have already set off to drive across Europe with it plus the heaviest furniture and props which cannot go by air.

At 11.00 on a Saturday night the company finishes its last performance at the Old Vic. At 8.00 the next morning the actors meet again at London Airport to catch the flight to Istanbul. The penalty for missing the plane is dismissal. There isn't another flight till Thursday.

Istanbul, Dubrovnik, Amman, Cairo . . . castles perched above the Bosphorous or the Adriatic, the backdrop of the Sphinx and the Pyramids. All this conjures up a picture of floodlit arenas beneath stars and velvet skies. The imagination does not fill in other details – the make-up running in the pouring sweat, under a costume weighing 20 pounds or more, in heat reaching 90 degrees even at night. These, and gastro-enteritis, were not the only local hazards of this tour.

In Dubrovnik, *Antony and Cleopatra* was played against the splendid backdrop of the Ducal Palace. In fact this meant performing at the end of a sealed-off street. The café next door to the palace stayed noisily open throughout and several hundred house martins roosting on the palace pillars were woken by the lights, decided it was dawn and kept up a deafening, screeching, twittering chorus, through which the actors had to shout to be heard.

In Split it was Diocletian's Palace which formed the setting – an all-too-solid palace when an actor going off stage left had to find his way through a maze of back streets and alleys in order to reappear stage right. One of the actors, finding his way blocked in an alley by three apparent thugs, had the presence of mind to draw his sword to put them to flight.

In Amman there were two kings in the audience, Hussein of Jordan and his guest, Constantine of Greece. Their presence required so many bodyguards that the actors had to push them aside to get on stage. Only 100 yards from the Sphinx (for the Cairo performance) was a night club pouring forth Arab music while the open ground of the stage poured forth ants, half an inch long, which marched purposefully up the inside of cloaks and costumes. And at Istanbul, the line 'The rest is silence' was answered by the mournful hooting of the ferries on the Bosphorous below.

Another diplomatic problem arose when Derek Jacobi's passport was found to contain an Israeli visa. He was hastily issued with a new one by the British Embassy to enable him to survive passport inspection at Cairo airport. So great was the hurry that the passport photograph had to be taken in the interval, which is why, for the next ten years, surprised immigration officials will be confronted with a picture of him in the lace collar and beard of Hamlet.

'You can't do any really serious acting against such distractions,' says John Nettleton, playing Polonius. 'Everything in the end is reduced to one strident note. There's no room for subtlety. All you can hope for is audibility and knowing where to get on and off.'

Edinburgh Festival

'It will be nice to get back to acting again,' Derek Jacobi says as they arrive back from the heat of Cairo to prepare to open the drama contribution to the Edinburgh Festival with *Antony and Cleopatra*. They have had four days off – the first since rehearsals started six months ago – during which most of them have caught colds. They arrive, oddly enough, to a setting just as makeshift and uncomfortable as the tents and castle dungeons they have toured and changed in around the Middle East: the gaunt, grey, stony Church of Scotland Assembly Hall, the parliament of the Elders of the Kirk.

Dorothy Tutin (Cleopatra) and Derek Jacobi (Octavius), with Suzanne Bertish (Iras)

One enters the Assembly Hall through an outer courtyard where the giant, robed and broad-brim-hatted statue of John Knox raises its threatening hand against the sort of frivolity and loose living he no doubt associated with strolling players. It is not an atmosphere friendly to drama. A temporary Elizabethan stage with a balcony and an inner curtained space beneath it is being hammered together in the hall itself – usually given over to ecclesiastical debate. Temporary amphitheatre seating has now been built over the pews, surrounding an apron stage that is a postage stamp compared with the arenas the actors have just been playing on.

Everything is makeshift once more. Pieces of unsecured balustrade topple over during rehearsal. Pillars wobble. The paint on the stairs is wet. And most of the entrances and exits have to be changed or adapted.

If the stage is improvised, backstage is like an army field dressing station just behind the lines. The Student's Common Room of the Divinity School, which normally occupies the building, is partitioned into dressing cubicles. In each narrow cell, four actors share a trestle table, a few mirrors and light bulbs and a row of coat-hooks on the wall. A few lucky ones have a wash-basin installed. The rest have to trek to the public lavatories outside the hall.

Meanwhile, perched above the cubicles, the company office from which the production is being controlled consists of three trestle tables and an ironing board . . . when the ironing board is not being used to press costumes just back from the cleaners. There is one telephone from which all the administration, press and radio coverage, and contact with the Festival authorities, is somehow being organised.

The costumes, which had been packed up still damp with sweat in the Middle East, and have now been cleaned and ironed, are still being mended by the wardrobe girls virtually as the actors climb into them for the public preview. 'It's going to look so cheap from this close,' mutters the designer, Nicholas Georgiadis, frowning from the front rows, which are only a foot or two from the stage. In fact the costumes, made out of cheap furnishing fabric from a London department store, look rich and magnificent – far more so than the balconied setting which was run up from a lorry-load of white timber which the company brought with it.

'I like this kind of sordid chaos really,' says Dorothy Tutin, making up as a bejewelled Cleopatra in front of a tiny mirror, with her belongings strewn round her on the floor. 'You are trying to make believe in terribly discouraging circumstances – which is what the actors of old had to do. I like it better than sitting in a proper dressing room, surrounded by flowers and telegrams and people telling you you will be marvellous when you know you're not. Carrie!' – she calls her dresser – 'Where are my rings? Haven't we got any better ones?' Carrie says she will go shopping tomorrow round Woolworths.

Two hours before the first night proper, Dorothy Tutin's voice is giving out. Pastilles and port and lemon are sent for. As the director gives his last notes to the cast, the balcony is still being adjusted, the downstage entrances through the auditorium are still being painted, music is still being changed and, as always, ASMs are sweeping the stage.

'We have got to get the feeling that time is running out for Antony,' says Toby Robertson sternly. 'Caesar is marching, events are overtaking him, he is a desperate man, a loser. If you can take five minutes out of the second half without gabbling you will have done it. Disintegration – that's what it's about.'

'That's what it's about all right,' wails Dorothy Tutin. 'My throat is disintegrating.'

After so many try-outs at home and abroad, that old first night adrenalin can still be sensed amid the hum of electric shavers and ceaseless traffic of people borrowing eye-liners and safety pins in the field dressing station. Does tonight feel different? – 'Yes, it does. Pulls you together,' says Alec McCowen, pulling on his cloak of gold thread and already barking in the

"The serpent of old Nile"

(next page) "Alas! poor Yorick"

style of Antony. 'Can I get you anything?' asks someone. 'Courage,' answers Derek Jacobi.

Over the partition a voice can be heard singing wordlessly, hopping between two notes like a bird. Dorothy Tutin is trying to encourage her voice.

Thanks to the inevitable parade of pipers holding up the traffic and the audience outside, the play begins late. The darkness banishes the feeling of a glorified church hall with its temporary scaffolding and plywood. The narrow space and the low, unimpressive balcony which must serve in quick succession as Rome, Alexandria, a ship of war and a monument, somehow helps to contain the sprawling play and put the imagination of the audience to work – as it must have done for Shakespeare's first audiences, piled into the Globe round a very similar acting area. The costumes, in effect, become the scenery. Their magnificence (even if obtained on the cheap) is not wasted.

Dorothy Tutin, scarcely able to speak on her first entrance, finds her voice once the first hurdle is past: the hoarseness was entirely psychological. Now she is using it to sound notes that she has never attempted at previous performances. You can feel confidence seeping back. Timothy West, who tore a ligament when his foot missed the stage in the Middle East, has turned his bandage and stick to good account as Enobarbus, who now stumps the stage leaning on a pole, an old soldier bearing his wounds doggedly. To everyone's surprise, the play has gone well.

How do actors unwind after three and a half hours strung up to this pitch? The 'darling-you-were-marvellous' scenes that the public imagines are impossible for a repertory company, which lives and works together much too closely to trade in hypocrisy. But it is necessary to be reassured afterwards, especially by the director, that the play has gone all right – or otherwise. 'I'll be giving notes tomorrow,' Toby Robertson adds to his congratulations.

After that, most people eat. Food, impossible before the performance, becomes the allayer of anxiety and the soother of nerves. And on tour in provincial Britain it is not easy to find at that hour. 'If you can just get a meal after you've finished work,' says Timothy West with feeling, 'you feel you've won a major battle.'

Bundling into Dorothy Tutin's small car, helter-skelter down from the Castle Heights of Edinburgh, they wind up, almost inevitably, at a Chinese restaurant. It is open. There is a burst of high spirits. Is this moment one of the 'highs' that addict actors to their work like a drug?

'I'm never really elated, whatever nice things people may say,' says Dorothy Tutin. 'The ultimate judge is really yourself – and you are always thinking of things that you should have done better. Sometimes you feel more like weeping.'

'There are nights of feeling elated but they're usually a bad sign,' says Alec McCowen. 'The performances you have enjoyed most are usually not very good ones. You have probably been too self-indulgent.'

But there must be times, surely, when an actor feels he has the audience in the palm of his hand? – 'Yes,' says Timothy West. 'And you'd be very foolish to assume that because it's happened, you've got them for the rest of the evening. An actor has always to be wary – or you lose them again without knowing it. If things are going well, one great satisfaction is to take a risk that you haven't taken before – a way of playing a certain thing – and then hear the audience confirm that it's come off.'

For anyone who still assumes that the life of a successful actor – as all these are – is one long ego trip, there is news. 'If you're left with one shred of self-respect at the end,' declares Dorothy Tutin, 'you're lucky. It's like being in a war. You feel that vulnerable. You never know what's going to hit you. In a company like this one, you feel you're going over the top. Yes,' she declaims proudly, 'we go over the top.'

'And isn't it wonderful?' says Timothy West, settling down to study the menu seriously. 'It's over. And we're all dead.'

Timothy West, with injured foot, as Enobarbus in Antony and Cleopatra

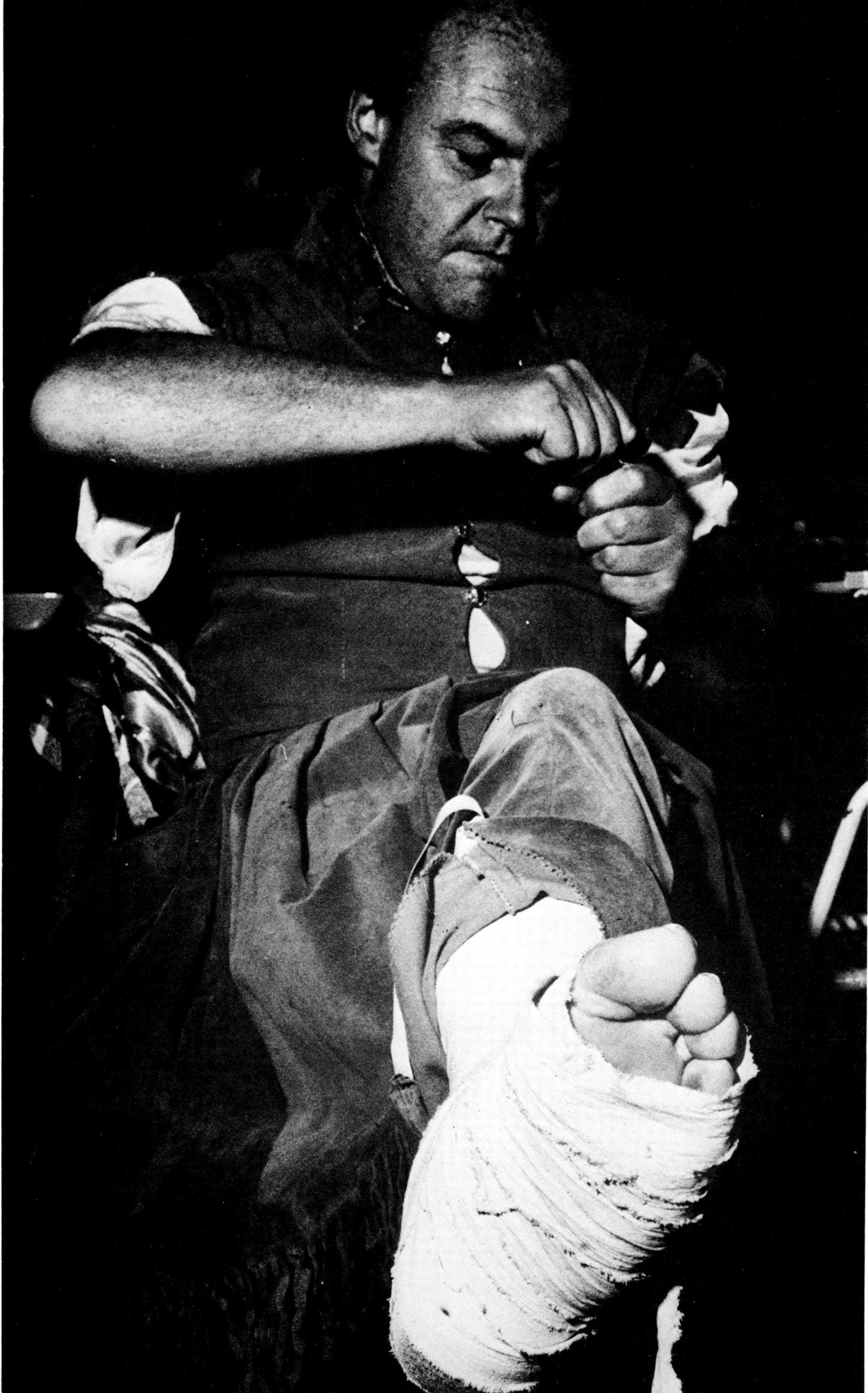

Glossary of Theatrical Terms.

Angels — *Financial backers of a show.*

A.S.M. — *Assistant Stage Manager.*

Backing — *Piece of scenery behind doors, windows or arches to hide the stage behind it.*

Batten — *Metal frame containing a row of unfocusable lamps.*

Beginners — *The actors who appear when each act begins.*

Bird, The — *Noisy expression of displeasure by audience, sometimes accompanied by missiles.*

Borders — *Lengths of plain cloth or canvas hung across the stage to mask the lighting bars or battens.*

Business — *All actions on stage, excluding gestures, such as opening a letter, preparing a meal.*

Cloth — *Any scene painted on canvas or net, battened top and bottom, to be hung or rolled up. If framed, it is a 'flat'.*

Comps (or Briefs) — *Complimentary tickets.*

Console — *The lighting control board.*

Corpse — *To break up with laughter, inappropriately, on stage.*

Counterweights — *The weights which enable scenery to be 'flown' in and out.*

Cover — *To cover a role is to understudy the actor playing it.*

Cueing — *Instructions given by stage manager or deputy for set and lighting changes by means of lights or hand signals or verbally.*

Cyclorama — *Stretched canvas backing, usually curved, representing sky or lit to a desired colour. 'Cyc' for short.*

Dates — *The successive Mondays on which a touring company is due to perform at various towns are their 'dates'.*

D.S.M. — *Deputy stage manager.*

Dock — *Storage area for scenery.*

Drapes — *Any soft material used for scenery.*

Dry	*When an actor forgets his lines, he 'dries'. Also 'a dry'.*
Electrics	*Electrical staff belonging to the theatre. LX for short.*
Equity	*Actors' trade union.*
Flies	*Area or gallery above and to the side of the stage where 'flying' pieces of scenery are controlled.*
Flop	*If a show is a flop, it 'bombs' or 'dies the death'. Also called a 'turkey'.*
Frocks	*Costumes, male or female.*
Front of House	*Every part of the theatre in front of the proscenium arch. F.O.H.*
Get-in	*To put scenery into a theatre. Hence 'the get-in' and 'the get-out' on tour.*
Go up	*To start the show, as is 'What time do we go up?' Similarly, 'Come down'.*
Green Room	*Actors' rest room backstage, usually with a canteen or bar.*
Grid	*Frame just below stage roof supporting pulley blocks by which scenery is flown.*
House	*A theatre building. Also the audience, as in 'A full house' or 'A good house'.*
House curtain	*The permanent curtain set behind the proscenium arch, also known as 'the tabs' or 'the rag'.*
Iron	*'The iron' is the fireproof safety curtain just behind the house curtain.*
Limes	*Follow-spots, manually operated to follow a character about the stage.*
Masking	*Hiding openings and lights from the view of the audience. Also when an actor downstage masks an actor upstage.*
Notices	*Newspaper critics' reviews.*
Practical	*Doors, windows and props which need to be in working condition are 'practical'.*
Prompt copy	*The typescript of the show complete with alterations and cues, also known as 'the book'.*

Prompt side	*Usually stage left when facing the audience from which the deputy stage manager gives all the cues.*
Properties	*Furniture and set dressing used for a scene. Personal articles carried but not worn by an actor are 'props' as distinct from costume.*
Proscenium	*The arch or border surrounding the stage. 'Pros' for short.*
Rake	*The angle of the stage rising to the back wall.*
Set	*The complete scenery for an act or scene. When all the props are set in position the play is 'set up'.*
Skip	*Travelling hamper for props or costumes.*
Stage cloth	*Painted canvas covering the floor of the stage.*
Strike	*To remove a scene or a prop from the stage.*
Study	*To learn the lines and examine the character one is to play. An actor may be known as 'a quick study'.*
Truck	*Heavy scenery placed on castors for quick movement.*
Walk-on	*A player who appears without lines or with very few.*
Wardrobe	*The costume department and staff, under the wardrobe mistress and wigmaster.*
Wings	*Flats set in rows along the sides of the stage. The hidden area at each side of the stage, behind them.*

On Tour 1977

Besides playing for 19 weeks in provincial towns in the United Kingdom, Prospect visited the following overseas places: The Hague, Brussels, Amsterdam, Luxemburg, Ludwigshafen, Gutersloh, Bonn, Bad Godesberg, Stuttgart, Dusseldorf, Duisburg, Hamburg, Ljubljana, Dubrovnik, Split, Istanbul, Amman, Cairo, and Teheran.

Prospect's London base is the world famous Old Vic Theatre.

The Company

Dave Atkins
Eileen Atkins
Suzanne Bertish
Philip Bloomfield
John Bowe
Karen Bowen
Paul Cartwright
Jeffrey Daunton
Robert Eddison
Graeme Elder
Donald Fraser
Rupert Frazer
Rosamond Freeman-Attwood
Kenneth Gilbert
Michael Howarth
Derek Jacobi
Emrys James
Barbara Jefford
Paul Jesson
Laurence Joyce
Charles Kay
Gary Kettel
Ronald Lacey
Anthony Langdon
William Lawford
Alan Lawrence
William Louther
Robert McBain
Neil McCaul
Alec McCowen
Peter Miles
John Nettleton
Geoffrey Palmer
Nigel Pratt
John Rowe
Robert Schofield
Terry Scully
Andr[illegible]ar
Davi[illegible]ghnessy
Paul Sherman
Bernice Stegers
Alice Stopczynski
Nick Stringer
Paul Vaughan-Teague
Frederick Treves
John Turner
Dorothy Tutin
Timothy West
Terence Wilton
Janis Winters
Philip York

HAMLET
Prince of Denmark
by William Shakespeare

Designed by	*Robin Archer*
Music by	*Donald Fraser*
Choreography by	*William Louther*
Fights by	*Ian McKay*
Lighting by	*Nick Chelton*
Directed by	*Toby Robertson*

HAMLET, Prince of Denmark
by William Shakespeare

Claudius, *King of Denmark*	**Timothy West**
Gertrude, *Queen of Denmark, mother to Hamlet*	**Barbara Jefford**
Hamlet, *son to the late, and nephew to the present King*	**Derek Jacobi**
Polonius, *Chamberlain to the King*	**John Nettleton**
Laertes, *his son*	**Terence Wilton**
Ophelia, *his daughter*	**Suzanne Bertish**
Voltimand } *Ambassadors*	**David Shaughnessy**
Cornelius } *Ambassadors*	**Jeffrey Daunton**
Horatio, *Friend of Hamlet*	**John Rowe**
Osric, *a Courtier*	**Neil McCaul**
Rosencrantz } *boy-hood friends of Hamlet*	**Michael Howarth**
Guildenstern } *boy-hood friends of Hamlet*	**Philip York**
Marcellus } *Soldiers*	**Kenneth Gilbert**
Barnardo } *Soldiers*	**Neil McCaul**
Francisco	**Jeffrey Daunton**
First Player } *In the dumbshow*	**John Turner**
Player King } *In the dumbshow*	**Graeme Edler**
Player Queen } *In the dumbshow*	**Alice Stopczynski**
Lucianus } *In the dumbshow*	**Rupert Frazer**
Player King } *In the play*	**Paul Vaughan Teague**
Player Queen } *In the play*	**Andrew Seear**
Lucianus } *In the play*	**John Turner**
First Gravedigger	**John Nettleton**
Second Gravedigger	**Paul Vaughan Teague**
Priest	**Kenneth Gilbert**
Sailors	**Philip Bloomfield** **Andrew Seear**
Fortinbras, *Prince of Norway*	**Rupert Frazer**
A Norwegian Captain	**Kenneth Gilbert**
Ghost of Hamlet's Father	**John Turner**
Musicians: Drums	**Paul Cartwright**
Trumpets	**Stephen Jenner**
Recorders	**Laurence Joyce**
Guitars	**Alan Lawrence**

Players, Courtiers, Soldiers
Graeme Edler, Karen Bowen, Rosamund Freeman-Attwood, Clive Gilbertson, Bernice Stegers, Alice Stopczynski and members of the Company.

For ***Hamlet***

Company Manager	Clare Fox
Stage Manager	Ted Irwin
Deputy Stage Manager	Garth Browne
Deputy Stage Manager	Ellen Grech
Deputy Stage Manager	Marje Williams
Assistant Stage Manager	Lance Campbell
Wardrobe Mistress	Vivienne Jenkins
Wig master	Robert Gardner
Armour	Richard Symons
Hats	Michael Jones, Fiona Willis
Costumes	June Callear, Sue Nightingale and the Wardrobe of Birmingham Repertory Theatre (Jennifer Adley: Hats), Dilys Elstone, Jean Lamprell, Susanna Owen, Jean Vickers, Lunita Williams
Boots and Shoes	Anello and Davide
Dyeing and painting of costumes	Gloria Wheeler, Mathilde Sandeberg, Josephine Lonergan
Additional props	Smallworks Ltd., John Campbell
Wigs	Wig Creations
Property Master	L. Erlich
Property Assistants	John Battye, Michael Jones, Anna Kerrigan
Weaponry	Alan Meek

The Dancers:
Karen Bowen, Graeme Edler, Rosamund Freeman-Attwood and Alice Stopczynski are founder members of the Dance and Theatre Corporation under the direction of William Louther.

Opening night at the New Theatre, Oxford, 19 April 1977

The Publishers wish to thank Prospect for their co-operation in producing this book.